Pop-Pop Nanu Opa Gramps Saba Sofu Pop-Pop Nanu Opa Gramps
Avô Grossvader Opi PawPaw Pappoús Avô Grossvader Opi PawPaw
Oppy Daada Papa Dadju Grampy Ded Oppy Daada Papa Dadju
Pepaw Aba Daddo Grandaddy Gompa Pepaw Aba Daddo Grandaddy
Geepa YeYe Gpa Farfar Afi Zeidy Pops Geepa YeYe Gpa Farfar Afi
Pop Bonpa Yeh Yeh Grand-papa Babu Pop Bonpa Yeh Yeh Grand-papa
Dedushka Jadd Kupuna Kane Grandpa Dedushka Jadd Kupuna Kane
Opa Halabeoji Grumpa Morfar Nonno Opa Halabeoji Grumpa Morfar
Ded Grossvader Opi Pappoús PawPaw Ded Grossvader Opi Pappoús
Poppie Jid Pepaw Ntatemogolo Papaw Poppie Jid Pepaw Ntatemogolo
Thatha Bubba Dziadzi Pepere Bestefar Thatha Bubba Dziadzi Pepere
Granddad Ong Deda Grandpop Chei Granddad Ong Deda Grandpop
Baba Abuelito Abuelo Cebuano Poppy Baba Abuelito Abuelo Cebuano

GRANDFATHER'S MEMORIES

A KEEPSAKE JOURNAL

This journal was given with gratitude to my grandfather

____

by his loving grandchild(ren)

____

A SPECIAL NOTE TO GRANDCHILDREN

Grandfathers are simply the best. It's a well-known fact. No one gives better hugs, brighter smiles, or more helpful advice. (And cookies, if you are lucky.) So how do you let your grandfather know how much you really appreciate him? One way is by giving him this special memory journal. There are prompts on its pages to help him tell his story, from the upper branches of his family tree all the way down to you. You will find out secrets, learn about family traditions, and appreciate what makes your grandfather such a treasure. You can read the journal together and ask even more questions about your grandfather's life and your place in a loving family. The memories and wisdom that your grandfather will share will make a wonderful and unique keepsake for you. The greatest gift a grandfather gives is his love, and each page will remind you of that. We sincerely hope you will enjoy giving and receiving this journal.

CONTENTS

MY FAMILY TREE

My Great-Grandfather

My Great-Grandfather

My Great-Grandmother

My Great-Grandmother

My Grandfather

My Grandmother

My Father

Me

My Sibling

My Sibling

My Great-Grandfather

My Great-Grandfather

My Great-Grandmother

My Great-Grandmother

My Grandfather

My Grandmother

My Mother

My Sibling

My Sibling

My Sibling

Chapter One

OUR FAMILY STORY

LOOK BACK, LEARN, AND LOVE

A FAMILY BEGINS

Our family names are ______________________

____

____

____

Here's what I know about our family names: ______________________

____

____

____

____

Our relatives came from ______________________

____

____

____

____

I learned about them through ______________________________

____

____

____

____

Some traditions we followed as a family were ______________________________

____

____

____

____

Here is an amazing story from our family's history: ______________________________

____

____

____

____

My family tree has many branches.
I cherish the memories that
make its roots run deep.

LYNDA I. FISHER

YOUR GREAT-GREATS

My grandparents were named ________________________________

____

____

But I called them ________________________________

____

____

This is my own grandfather's story: ________________________

____

____

____

____

____

____

____

My other grandparent has a story, too: ______________________

____

____

____

____

____

____

This is how they met, where they lived, and what they did: ______________________

____

____

____

____

____

____

____

That is your legacy on this Earth when you leave this Earth: how many hearts you have touched.

PATTI DAVIS

Something I'd like to tell you about my grandfather is

Words I would use to describe my other grandparent:

Things I remember the most about my grandparents:

Ways you remind me of them:

YOUR GREATS

My parents were named

But I called them

My brothers and sisters were

This is my father's story:

This is my other parent's history: ____________________

They met when ____________________

The places they lived were ____________________

A happier man you will never see than he, whenever he can get his great-grandchildren on his knee.

CHARLES LAMB

My parents' jobs were ______________________________

____

And ______________________________

____

But they really enjoyed doing ______________________________

____

And ______________________________

____

Here's what our family life was like: ______________________________

____

____

____

____

____

____

One thing our family loved to do together was

What I'd like you to know about my father:

What I want to share about my other parent:

The things they passed down to me were

A memory to share from when I was your age:

WHEN I WAS BORN

I was born on ____

The day of the week was __________________________________

In a place called ______________________________________

My full name is _______________________________________

My parents chose it because _______________________________

As a baby, I was ______________________________________

Here are the people who lived with us, and their dates of birth: ____________________

The two most important days in your life are the day you were born, and the day you find out why.

MARK TWAIN

Chapter Two

ALL ABOUT ME

MY STORY TO SHARE WITH YOU

WHERE THE HEART IS

The place I lived when I was a little boy was ______________________________

____

____

____

____

____

My first memories of home were ______________________________

____

____

____

____

____

____

____

Let me tell you about my room: ______________________________

____

____

____

____

We had pets named ______________________________

____

____

____

____

Something yummy we ate together was ______________________________

____

____

____

____

A house is made with walls and beams;
a home is built with love and dreams.

RALPH WALDO EMERSON

The friends I played with were

My favorite things to do were

I loved going to the

The best place to hide was

Here is a story from when I was little:

STARTING SCHOOL

My first day at school was ______________________________

____

____

____

The school was called ______________________________

____

____

____

____

Here's how I got there: ______________________________

____

____

____

____

My first teacher was called

My favorite school outfit was

And I always carried

Education is the key to unlocking the world, a passport to freedom.

OPRAH WINFREY

Memories from my earliest years at school:

MOVING UP

I started middle school in ______________________________

____

____

____

My school was named ______________________________

____

____

____

____

The subjects I liked learning were ______________________________

____

____

____

____

And the ones I didn't like so much were ____

____

____

____

____

Everybody said I was good at ____

____

____

____

____

My best friends were ____

____

____

____

____

One child, one teacher, one pen, and one book can change the world.

MALALA YOUSAFZAI

Let me tell you some stories from this time:

SCHOOL'S OUT

The things I liked to do after school were ______

My hobbies were ______

When I was naughty and when I was nice: ______________________

____

____

____

____

____

The best snacks were ______________________

____

____

____

____

My after-school friends were named ______________________

____

____

____

Be curious, not cool.

KEN BURNS

Weekends were special because ______________________

During winter breaks I used to ______________________

I looked forward to summer vacation because ______________________

My best vacation was

This is how I loved to spend my ideal day out of school:

HELLO, HIGH SCHOOL

I went to high school at ______________________________

____

____

The subjects I enjoyed most were ______________________________

____

____

____

I spent a lot of time watching the clock in this class: ______________________________

____

____

My friends were ______________________________

____

____

____

We liked to ______________________________

____

____

____

My school activities included ______________________________

____

____

____

My favorite after-school snack was ______________________________

____

____

My go-to outfit for school ______________________________

____

____

____

If you believe in yourself and
with a tiny pinch of magic,
all your dreams can come true.

SPONGEBOB SQUAREPANTS

Here's how I would describe myself during my high school years:

MY TIME AS A TEENAGER

When I was a teenager, I was crazy about ________________________

My favorite kind of music was ________________________

I used to listen to it on my ________________________

An instrument I learned how to play: ______________________________

____

____

____

____

The songs that spoke to me as a teenager: ______________________________

____

____

____

____

Musicians I loved and went to see were ______________________________

____

____

____

____

With confidence, you have won before you have started.

MARCUS GARVEY

The best books and authors were ______________________________

My favorite character from a book was ______________________________

Some of the movies I loved were ______________________________

My favorite movie theater snack ______________________________

My favorite television shows were ______________________________

I never, ever missed an episode of ______________________________

My best friends were

Like most teenagers, we used to wear

One thing I will never wear again is

How I wore my hair:

The things we thought were cool were

But definitely not

My favorite way to spend time was

I had jobs like

Someone who had a big influence on me was

Because

If you met me as a teenager, you would see

The bravest thing I did was

Here's a secret your parents might not even know about me:

Here's something important I learned when I was a teenager:

HIGHER LEARNING

I went to college at ______________________________

____

____

____

I chose this college because ______________________________

____

____

____

____

____

My college tuition at the time cost ______________________________

____

____

____

I went to school to study ____________________

____

____

____

____

____

____

____

I got a degree in ____________________

____

____

____

____

____

____

There is no elevator to success.
You have to take the stairs.

ZIG ZIGLAR

My best friends in college were

One of my most memorable experiences was

Something I learned about myself I didn't know: ____________________

Advice I would give you about going to college: ____________________

Chapter Three

MAKING MEMORIES

LIFE ON MY OWN

ON MY WAY

Here's what I did after finishing school: ______

My new home was in ______

The things that were important to me were ______________________

____

____

____

____

____

____

The hopes and wishes I had for the future were ____________________

____

____

____

____

____

____

____

Living alone makes it harder to find someone to blame.

MASON COOLEY

How I stayed in touch with my parents: ______________________

____

____

____

____

____

The first thing I did when returning to my childhood home was ______________________

____

____

____

____

____

How living on my own helped me to understand my family better: ______________________

____

____

____

____

____

Here's something I learned from that time to share with you: ______________________

CLIMBING THE LADDER

My first grown-up job was ______________________________

____

____

____

This is what I did: ______________________________

____

____

____

____

____

This is how much I made a week or a month: ______________

____

____

____

Some of the best things about the job were

But, to be honest, I could have done without the

The only way to do great work is to love what you do. If you haven't found it yet, keep looking.

STEVE JOBS

Every job is a learning experience, and I found out that

The next jobs I held were

One job that I will never forget was

What I was really hoping to do was ______________________________

____

____

____

____

____

____

____

____

If I could go back and change something about that time, it would be ______________________________

____

____

____

____

____

____

____

____

MAKING A HOME

How I felt making my own home for the first time: ______________________

____

____

____

____

Where I lived was ______________________

____

____

How much my rent or mortgage was: ______________________

____

____

The view from my window was ______________________

____

____

My favorite room was ________________________________

____

____

Something I brought from my parents' house was ________________

____

____

A keepsake I still have from that time is ____________________

____

____

Some of the other places I lived were _______________________

____

____

I started to feel like a grown-up when ______________________

____

____

"Home" is the nicest word there is.

LAURA INGALLS WILDER

GOOD TIMES

Here's how I loved to spend my free time: ______________________________

____

____

____

Would you find me outdoors or in? ______________________________

____

My social life was ______________________________

____

____

____

Good friends included ______________________________

____

____

____

The places I loved to visit were ________________________________

____

____

____

My top three movies were ________________________________

____

____

____

Three favorite songs I played on repeat: ________________________________

____

____

____

Bet you didn't know I could dance the ________________________________

____

____

Start your twenties with a lot of good friends and leave with a few good ones.

RYAN O'CONNELL

I never left home without ______________________________

____

____

____

My go-to weekend outfit was ______________________________

____

____

____

And one I'd rather not be seen in now was ______________________________

____

____

____

I got around by ______________________________

____

____

____

Something new I tried or learned was

No weekend was complete without

LOVE IS ALL YOU NEED

Where and when I first met my partner/spouse: ______________________

____

____

The first thing I noticed was ______________________

____

____

____

____

Here's the true story of how we met: ______________________

____

____

____

____

____

Our very first date was ______________________________

____

____

____

____

____

____

There was a second date because ______________________________

____

____

____

____

We dated for ______________________________

____

____

When life gives you something very special, you don't have to dream anymore.

UNKNOWN

The most fun we had together was ______________________________

One time I'd rather forget was ______________________________

When I first met my partner's/spouse's family: ______________________

The moment I fell in love: ______________________

How we committed to each other: ______________________

TYING THE KNOT

Where and when we made it official: ______________________________

____

____

____

Some of our guests were ______________________________

____

____

____

____

Let me tell you about what we wore: ______________________________

____

____

____

____

The things I will remember forever about that day are ______________________

____

____

____

____

Something funny also happened that day: ______________________________

____

____

____

____

Our hopes and dreams for a life together were ______________________

____

____

____

____

My most brilliant achievement was my ability to be able to persuade my wife to marry me.

WINSTON CHURCHILL

A LIFE TOGETHER

How our life together began: ______________________________

____

____

Our first home together was ______________________________

____

____

We were best friends with ______________________________

____

____

____

Some of the things we liked to do were ______________________________

____

____

____

How being together changed me:

Here is a story from that special time:

Marriage is not just spiritual communion, it is also remembering to take out the trash.

DR. JOYCE BROTHERS

Chapter Four

TIMES TO TREASURE

WELCOMING YOUR PARENT TO THE WORLD

HELLO, BABY!

When I found out I was pregnant with your parent, I felt ______________________

____

____

____

____

We were living at ____

____

We welcomed your parent at ____

____

____

The first time we saw your parent, we __________________________________

____

____

____

Here's a little bit more about the day your parent was born: ______________________

____

____

____

____

____

We named your parent ______________________________

____

Because ______________________________________

____

____

____

And your parent's nickname was __________________________

____

____

A father is a man who expects his son to be as good a man as he meant to be.

FRANK A. CLARK

My memories of your parent as a tiny baby:

STARTING TO GROW

How I would describe your parent as a young child: ______________________

____

____

____

____

Other people in your parent's family, before and after, were ______________________

____

____

____

____

A person who looked after your parent was ______________________

____

____

____

Who your parent looked like: ______________________________

____

____

____

What my parents had to say about your parent: ______________________________

____

____

____

____

Let me tell you how I felt as a new father: ______________________________

____

____

____

____

____

*Of all the titles I've been privileged to have,
Dad has always been the best.*

KEN NORTON

Stories, songs, and books your parent loved are

An activity your parent never got enough of was

Places your parent loved to go:

Favorite games were

Foods your parent found yummy were

The best toys were

Your parent could not go to sleep without

Some of my special memories of your parent as a child (and some funny and embarrassing ones, too!) are

READY FOR SCHOOL

Your parent's first school was ______________________________

____

Here's how I remember the first day: ______________________

____

____

____

____

____

Your parent got to school by ______________________________

____

____

After school, your parent always __________________________

____

____

Sports, clubs, and hobbies your parent was involved in:

Let me tell you about your parent's report cards in those early years:

Wisdom begins in wonder.

SOCRATES

GROWING UP

Your parent went to middle school at ______________________________

____

____

What your parent liked about school was ______________________________

____

____

____

____

Something that was not so popular was ______________________________

____

____

____

____

____

After school, you could find your parent ____

____

____

____

I remember a funny story from that time: ____

____

____

____

____

Your parent's best friend was ____

____

____

____

____

____

We try to teach our children all about life. Our children teach us what life is all about.

ANGELA SCHWINDT

FAMILY FUN

The things we always did as a family included ______________________________

____

____

____

____

Our favorite weekends together always had ______________________________

____

____

____

____

The pets we had were ______________________________

____

____

____

During the summer, we would

Here's how your parent got along with the rest of the family:

Let me tell you a funny story your parent will never share:

If you want to change the world, go home and love your family.

MOTHER THERESA

TEEN TIMES

As a teenager, your parent couldn't get enough of ______________________________

____

____

Your parent liked to wear ____

____

____

The music coming through the bedroom door was usually ______________________

____

____

And let me describe that bedroom: ____

____

____

____

____

Your parent made me proud when ______________________________

____

____

____

____

____

But I was a little annoyed when ______________________________

____

____

____

Your parent's personality was like yours in this way: ______________________________

____

____

____

____

Be yourself; everyone else is already taken.

OSCAR WILDE

Let me tell you all about your parent's experience in high school:

Here are some other stories I'd like to share about when your parent was a teenager:

FLYING THE NEST

Your parent's dream for the future after school was

What your parent did, and where:

Here is what I remember about the first time your parent left home:

What I missed the most was ______________________________

____

____

____

____

Something I didn't really miss was ______________________________

____

____

____

____

I knew your parent was really growing up when ______________________________

____

____

____

____

Where we love is home. Home that our feet may leave but not our hearts.

OLIVER WENDELL HOLMES, SR.

YOUR PARENTS MEET

Your parents met at ______________________________

____

____

____

Here's what happened the first time I met your other parent: ______________________________

____

____

____

____

What surprised me was ______________________________

____

____

____

____

I thought this might be a special relationship when ________________

____

____

____

____

____

Let me tell you a story from the time your parents met: ________________

____

____

____

____

____

____

____

____

Who ever loved that loved not at first sight?

William Shakespeare

Here are my memories about when your parents decided to make a life with each other:

BIG NEWS

When I found out you were going to be born, I ____________________

____

____

____

____

____

____

This is how I got the news: ____________________

____

____

____

____

____

____

When you appeared, I was ____________________

____

____

____

____

This is how I first met you: ____________________

____

____

____

____

I couldn't help feeling ____________________

____

____

____

____

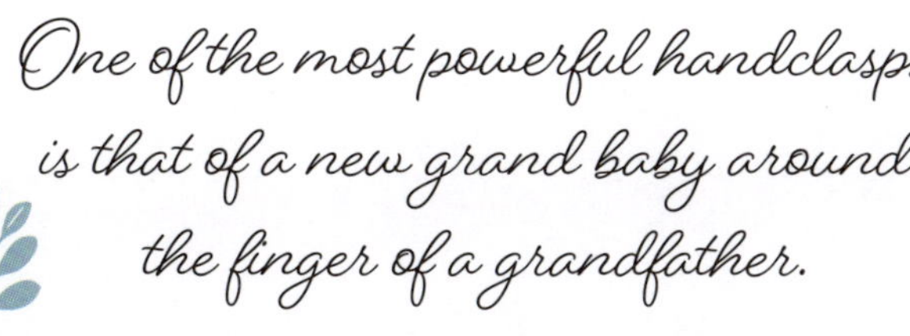

One of the most powerful handclasps is that of a new grand baby around the finger of a grandfather.

JOY HARGROVE

Chapter Five

FROM ME TO YOU

BECOMING YOUR GRANDFATHER

WELCOME TO THE FAMILY

My memories of your first few months are

This is how your father was: ______________________________

____

____

This is how your other parent was: ______________________________

____

____

A funny question about babies they had for me was ______________________________

____

____

____

This is what it felt like to hold you: ______________________________

____

____

____

____

Only the best dads get promoted to grandpa.

UNKNOWN

YOU REMIND ME

You were grandchild number ______________________

____

The family member you reminded me of is ______________________

____

Because ______________________

____

____

____

I think you looked like ______________________

____

Because ______________________

____

____

____

Here are the ways you remind me of your own parent: ______

A grandfather is someone you can look up to no matter how tall you grow.

UNKNOWN

YOU AS A BABY

This is how I would describe you as a baby:

Everyone else in the family thought

One thing that made your own personality shine through was

One of the best memories from that time is

Just when you think you know all that love is, along come the grandchildren.

UNKNOWN

YOUR PARENTS AS PARENTS

These are the things your father loved about having a baby:

And your other parent felt

If they came to me about advice, it was

Grandfathers do have a special place in the lives of their children's children.

ALVIN POUSSAINT

ME AS A GRANDFATHER

This is how I felt about becoming a grandfather: ______________________

This is what surprised me the most: ______________________

A special gift I gave you when you were tiny was ______________________

____

I chose it because ______________________________

____

____

____

____

Things I learned as a grandfather, to pass on to you: ______________

____

____

____

____

____

____

____

A grandfather is someone with silver in his hair and gold in his heart.

UNKNOWN

This is a place to collect special memories between just you and me:

MY HOPES AND DREAMS

After you appeared in our family life, I wanted the most wonderful future for you. This is what I was thinking about:

Grandfathers bring a little wisdom,
happiness, warmth, and love
to every life they touch.

UNKNOWN

Chapter Six

OUR TRADITIONS

THE RITUALS AND RECIPES THAT MAKE US A FAMILY

FAMILY HERITAGE

Our family's nationality is ____________________

____

____

____

Our ethnic background is ____________________

____

____

____

____

Here are some of the places your ancestors came from: ____________________

____

____

____

____

Some traditions we followed from our ethnic heritage were ________________

____

____

____

____

We also followed these religious traditions: ________________

____

____

____

____

They are important to us because ________________

____

____

____

____

There are only two lasting bequests
we can give to our children—
one is roots, the other is wings.

HODDING S. CARTER

GATHERING TOGETHER

Our shared family beliefs include ______

Some of the holiday traditions we follow include ______

The holidays that have always meant the most to our family have been

Our family usually gets together when

A tradition is kept alive only by something being added to it.

HENRY JAMES

Let me tell you about some of the amazing times our family got together:

FOOD FOR THOUGHT

Traditional family dishes that we ate were ______________________________

____

____

____

Something I remember about family meals when growing up: ______________

____

____

____

____

Our family had rules about dinnertime: ______________________________

____

____

____

____

Some of the foods we ate on special occasions were ______________________

____

____

____

____

____

Here are some family members and their special dishes: ______________________

____

____

____

____

____

____

____

____

After a good dinner one can forgive anybody, even one's own relatives.

OSCAR WILDE

FAMILY RECIPES

Here are some of the family recipes we've loved to make and eat over the years:

Recipe: ______________________________

Ingredients:

______________________ ______________________

______________________ ______________________

______________________ ______________________

______________________ ______________________

Instructions: ______________________________

____

____

____

____

____

____

Recipe: ____________________

Ingredients:

Instructions: ____________________

Cooking with love provides food for the soul.

UNKNOWN

SPECIAL HOLIDAY RECIPES

On holidays and special times, you could always find on the table:

Recipe: ______________________________

Ingredients:

______________________________ ______________________________

______________________________ ______________________________

______________________________ ______________________________

______________________________ ______________________________

Instructions: ______________________________

____

____

____

____

____

____

Recipe: ______________________________

Ingredients:

______________________ ______________________

______________________ ______________________

______________________ ______________________

______________________ ______________________

Instructions: ______________________________

MY RECIPE FOR HAPPINESS

Just for you, here is grandfather's recipe for happiness:

Recipe: ______________________________

Ingredients:

______________________________ ______________________________

______________________________ ______________________________

______________________________ ______________________________

______________________________ ______________________________

Instructions: ______________________________

____

____

____

____

____

____

Recipe: ______________________________

Ingredients:

______________________________ ______________________________

______________________________ ______________________________

______________________________ ______________________________

______________________________ ______________________________

Instructions: ______________________________

____

____

____

____

____

____

____

____

Happiness is having what you want and wanting what you have.

JOSH BILLINGS

Bluestreak

An imprint of Weldon Owen International.

www.weldonowen.com

ISBN: 978-1-68188-642-8

PRINTED IN CHINA

10 9 8 7 6 5 4 3 2 1

Pop-Pop Nanu Opa Gramps Saba Sofu Pop-Pop Nanu Opa Gramps S
vô Grossvader Opi PawPaw Pappoús Avô Grossvader Opi PawPaw Pa
Oppy Daada Papa Dadju Grampy Ded Oppy Daada Papa Dadju Grar
paw Aba Daddo Grandaddy Gompa Pepaw Aba Daddo Grandaddy Go
Geepa YeYe Gpa Farfar Afi Zeidy Pops Geepa YeYe Gpa Farfar Afi Ze
op Bonpa Yeh Yeh Grand-papa Babu Pop Bonpa Yeh Yeh Grand-papa
Dedushka Jadd Kupuna Kane Grandpa Dedushka Jadd Kupuna Kane
pa Halabeoji Grumpa Morfar Nonno Opa Halabeoji Grumpa Morfar N
ed Grossvader Opi Pappoús PawPaw Ded Grossvader Opi Pappoús Pa
Poppie Jid Pepaw Ntatemogolo Papaw Poppie Jid Pepaw Ntatemogol
tha Bubba Dziadzi Pepere Bestefar Thatha Bubba Dziadzi Pepere Bes
Granddad Ong Deda Grandpop Chei Granddad Ong Deda Grandp
ba Abuelito Abuelo Cebuano Poppy Baba Abuelito Abuelo Cebuano

Pop-Pop Nanu Opa Gramps Saba Sofu Pop-Pop Nanu Opa Gramps S
vô Grossvader Opi PawPaw Pappoús Avô Grossvader Opi PawPaw Pa
Oppy Daada Papa Dadju Grampy Ded Oppy Daada Papa Dadju Grar
paw Aba Daddo Grandaddy Gompa Pepaw Aba Daddo Grandaddy Go
Geepa YeYe Gpa Farfar Afi Zeidy Pops Geepa YeYe Gpa Farfar Afi Ze
op Bonpa Yeh Yeh Grand-papa Babu Pop Bonpa Yeh Yeh Grand-papa
Dedushka Jadd Kupuna Kane Grandpa Dedushka Jadd Kupuna Kane
pa Halabeoji Grumpa Morfar Nonno Opa Halabeoji Grumpa Morfar
ed Grossvader Opi Pappoús PawPaw Ded Grossvader Opi Pappoús P
Poppie Jid Pepaw Ntatemogolo Papaw Poppie Jid Pepaw Ntatemogo
tha Bubba Dziadzi Pepere Bestefar Thatha Bubba Dziadzi Pepere Be
Granddad Ong Deda Grandpop Chei Granddad Ong Deda Grand
ba Abuelito Abuelo Cebuano Poppy Baba Abuelito Abuelo Cebuano
Pop-Pop Nanu Opa Gramps Saba Sofu Pop-Pop Nanu Opa Gramps S
vô Grossvader Opi PawPaw Pappoús Avô Grossvader Opi PawPaw P
Oppy Daada Papa Dadju Grampy Ded Oppy Daada Papa Dadju Gra
paw Aba Daddo Grandaddy Gompa Pepaw Aba Daddo Grandaddy G
Geepa YeYe Gpa Farfar Afi Zeidy Pops Geepa YeYe Gpa Farfar Afi Ze
op Bonpa Yeh Yeh Grand-papa Babu Pop Bonpa Yeh Yeh Grand-pap
Dedushka Jadd Kupuna Kane Grandpa Dedushka Jadd Kupuna Kane
pa Halabeoji Grumpa Morfar Nonno Opa Halabeoji Grumpa Morfar
ed Grossvader Opi Pappoús PawPaw Ded Grossvader Opi Pappoús P
Poppie Jid Pepaw Ntatemogolo Papaw Poppie Jid Pepaw Ntatemogo
tha Bubba Dziadzi Pepere Bestefar Thatha Bubba Dziadzi Pepere Be
Granddad Ong Deda Grandpop Chei Granddad Ong Deda Grand